# WISHES ARE MEDICINE!

## HOW MAKE-A-WISH® GAVE ME HOPE & HELPED ME HEAL

BY
JAMIE HEATH

ADAPTED AND
ILLUSTRATED BY
LEONARD WELLS KENYON

THIS BOOK IS DEDICATED TO
ALL THOSE WHO SUPPORTED
ME ALONG THE WAY!

– JAMIE HEATH

Edited By James Hathaway, Casey McMorrow,
Shawna Wakeham-Smith, and Beth Barnes

Book layout, art, cover and design by Leonard Wells Kenyon.
www.leonardkenyon.com

Printed by Springfield Printing Company, Inc.
19 Precision Drive, North Springfield, VT. 05150

Make-A-Wish® Vermont
The Vermont Teddy Bear Factory
6655 Shelburne Road Suite 300 Shelburne, Vermont 05482.
802.864.9393
www.vermont.wish.org

ISBN-13: 978-0-692-14508-1

I WASN'T FEELING WELL.

MAY

APRIL

DECEMBER

JUNE

MARCH

NEWS ROOM

THE TURTLES SWIM!

Refer a child www.vermont.wish.org    Refer a child www.vermont.wish.org

FOR A
LONG
TIME.

I HAD TO
**LEARN**
HOW TO
**WALK**
**AGAIN!**

AND EVEN
TO
READ!

IT WAS
SLOW
GOING.

I MOVED
LIKE A
TURTLE.

ACTUALLY, MY PET TURTLE, BOB, WAS FASTER!

. . . WHERE I DID NOT WANT TO GET OUT OF BED!

THEN ONE
DAY, TWO
WONDERFUL
PEOPLE CAME
TO VISIT.

THEY WERE WISH GRANTERS!

THEY WEREN'T REAL WIZARDS
OR FAIRY GODMOTHERS!
THEY WERE FROM
# MAKE-A-WISH
AND THEY'D COME TO GRANT ME A WISH!

SO
MANY
. . .

. . . POSSIBILITIES!

BOB HAD A PLAN OF HIS OWN.

HE GRABBED MY FAVORITE BOOK

AND GOT MY ATTENTION.

THEN IT CAME TO ME! I WISHED TO SWIM WITH SEA TURTLES.

THEN
THE DAY
FINALLY
CAME!

AND . . .

...IT
WAS
AMAZING!

SINCE MY WISH,
THINGS JUST KEPT
GETTING BETTER!

I PLAY
SPORTS
AGAIN!

I'VE MET
CELEBRITIES
AND BEEN ON TV!

I EVEN
DRIVE!

TO BE CONTINUED . . .

WHAT WOULD
YOU
WISH FOR?

Dr. First: Chief of Pediatrics, University of Vermont Children's Hospital.

# DOCTOR'S NOTE

Building strengths and resiliencies in children like Jamie, the author of this book, is a key reason I became a pediatrician. It may surprise you to know that Jamie did not create a fictional character but wrote this story based on her own life experience. Her inability to walk and read was due to her experiencing two major episodes of bleeding into her brain due to abnormally formed blood vessels in her head. The effect of such a disability can certainly depress any person, let alone a child, and hamper their drive to overcome whatever their health challenge is, despite the medical and rehabilitative treatments available.

In fact, if a child is going to overcome a disability or disease as Jamie eventually did, the mind and body of that child need to work together and like the sea turtles in the book, create a desire to never give up. That is where Make-A-Wish Vermont comes into play as a critical part of the healing process. Having a wish granted by Make-A-Wish Vermont is truly transformational and in turn transforms not just the child, but the child's family, friends, and all of us on that child's health care team. That is what happened to Jamie, who is now doing well, as she tells us at the end of the story. That is what the power of a wish is all about.

*Lewis R First*

- Dr. Lewis First

## TO REFER A CHILD PLEASE VISIT: WWW.VERMONT.WISH.ORG/REFER-A-CHILD

tO Do:
Turtle Food.
Organize Desk
Vet Trip – (Tell Bob we are
going for icecream)
get Sand out of mY suitcase!

## JAMIE HEATH

Since writing *Wishes are Medicine,* Jamie graduated Summa Cum Laude from Norwich University with a Bachelor's Degree in Business Technology and Management. After graduation, Jamie joined the Make-A-Wish® Vermont team as the Wish and Marketing Manager. She coordinates the Wish Ambassador program and participates in the Wish Discovery process, helping Wish Kids determine their wishes. This book plays a big role in that process. She also serves as a Wish Ambassador speaking at events and signing books.

In Jamie's free time, you can catch her at the pool coaching swim teams or swimming herself.

At her request, all proceeds of *Wishes are Medicine* are donated to **Make-A-Wish® Vermont.**

## LEONARD WELLS KENYON
### (Lenny K.)

Leonard is an author and illustator from Vermont. His works include ***BIG UGLY***, ***How to Scare a Monster!***, ***A World Without Color***, ***Vermont Magazine,*** and more.
For more, please visit: **leonardkenyon.com**

Friends for Life:
Make-A-Wish® Vermont, President & CEO, James Hathaway & Jamie Heath